Ratites can be found on all continents south of the equator except Antarctica. At least partly, the places where these birds live have shaped the way they look and behave. For instance, rheas and ostriches live on different continents and are only distantly related—yet they look and act very much alike. This is partly because they both live on grasslands, where long necks help them look for predators and long legs help them run fast to escape.

Emus and cassowaries are more closely related—yet they don't look much alike. Cassowaries have hard crowns on their heads and shield-like quills on their bodies. These protect them from dense underbrush in the forests. The tall emus live on the open deserts and have long legs (like ostriches) to help them run from enemies. Kiwis are night hunters. They have special senses to help them find food in the dark. The most common species for each ratite family are shown below.

EMU
Dromaius novaehollandiae

The emu lives in the deserts and woodlands of Australia. It has loose, downy feathers that droop in the back to form a mop-like "tail." Its bluish skin becomes darker or lighter in color, depending on its mood.

SOUTHERN CASSOWARY
Casuarius casuarius

The cassowary lives in the tropical rain forests of Australia, New Guinea, and nearby islands. Its shiny black feathers hang loosely from its body, and look more like hair than like feathers! Like turkeys, most cassowaries have long flaps of skin hanging from their throats. These flaps are called *wattles*.

BROWN KIWI
Apteryx australis

The kiwi lives in the forests of New Zealand. Although it can see fairly well, it is also one of the few birds with a good sense of smell. And it is the *only* bird in the world whose nostrils open at the tip of the bill.

NORTH AFRICAN OSTRICH
Struthio camelus camelus

The ostrich is found only in Africa, although at one time it also lived on the deserts of Arabia. Ostriches have broad, flat bills and long necks. They are often called camel birds. This may be because of their long eyelashes, their long necks—or because, like camels, they can live on deserts.

COMMON RHEA
Rhea americana

Rheas roam the open grasslands of South America. Gray-brown and white in color, they are sometimes called "South American ostriches."

The body of a ratite is built for running instead of flying. Ostriches and rheas, for example, have small wings that could never lift their heavy bodies off the ground. But their long, muscular legs enable them to run very fast, taking long strides as they go. And their excellent senses help them find food and tell them when danger is near. Although ratites don't use their wings for flying, they do use them for other purposes. Cassowaries use their stiff wings as shields when moving through the sharp undergrowth. Emus use their wings to shade their nests. And kiwis tuck their heads under their wings when they sleep.

When they need to, ostriches use the spurs on the ends of their wings to fight off enemies.

To fly, a bird needs powerful muscles to move its wings. These muscles can develop only if there is a big, strong *keel* (raised area on the breastbone) to which the muscles can attach.

FLYING BIRD

Ratites have flat, smooth breastbones. They do *not* have keels. With no big bone to attach to, their wing muscles are small and not powerful enough for flight.

RATITE

Ratites have powerful running muscles to hel them escape from predators, such as big cats, dogs, and other large mammals. When running at full speed, ostriches and rheas use their wings like sails. They can change direction quickly by raising one wing and lowering the other.

OSTRICH   RHEA   MAN   KIWI   CASSOWARY   EMU

Living on the ground has allowed most ratites to grow big, and their large size can scare away predators. The ostrich is the world's biggest bird. The emu is second in size among living birds. The common rhea is the largest bird in the Americas.

4

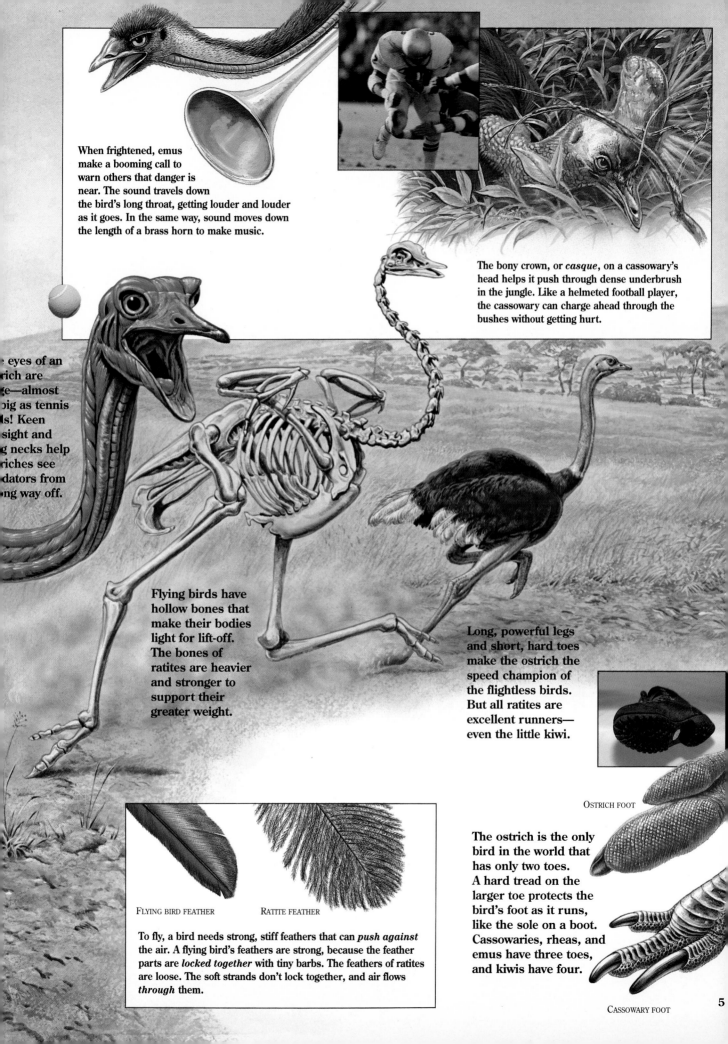

When frightened, emus make a booming call to warn others that danger is near. The sound travels down the bird's long throat, getting louder and louder as it goes. In the same way, sound moves down the length of a brass horn to make music.

The bony crown, or *casque*, on a cassowary's head helps it push through dense underbrush in the jungle. Like a helmeted football player, the cassowary can charge ahead through the bushes without getting hurt.

e eyes of an
rich are
e—almost
big as tennis
ls! Keen
sight and
g necks help
riches see
dators from
ng way off.

Flying birds have hollow bones that make their bodies light for lift-off. The bones of ratites are heavier and stronger to support their greater weight.

Long, powerful legs and short, hard toes make the ostrich the speed champion of the flightless birds. But all ratites are excellent runners— even the little kiwi.

OSTRICH FOOT

The ostrich is the only bird in the world that has only two toes. A hard tread on the larger toe protects the bird's foot as it runs, like the sole on a boot. Cassowaries, rheas, and emus have three toes, and kiwis have four.

FLYING BIRD FEATHER   RATITE FEATHER

To fly, a bird needs strong, stiff feathers that can *push against* the air. A flying bird's feathers are strong, because the feather parts are *locked together* with tiny barbs. The feathers of ratites are loose. The soft strands don't lock together, and air flows *through* them.

CASSOWARY FOOT

5

Birds probably started flying as a way to escape from enemies. A flying bird can quickly move out of reach of a hungry predator. So flight is a powerful tool of survival. Scientists tell us that some ratites may have lost the power of flight because they had no enemies. Birds living on islands without predators may not have needed to fly. Over time, they developed other ways of traveling, such as running and swimming. And when enemies *did* invade their homes, ratites developed strong leg muscles to outrun them.

As far back as 100 million years ago, some birds could fly and some could not. And some became *extinct*, or died out, while others survived. Nobody knows for sure why some flightless birds became extinct. Scientists think that predators, including humans, may have killed them off. Others may have died out when the climate of their habitats changed.

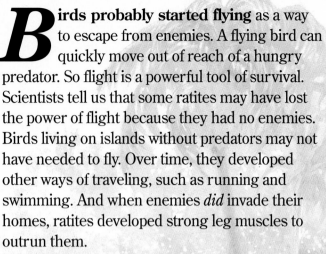

By flying, birds can escape predators on the ground. A charging lion can't follow a bird into the air, so the air is a safe space.

A flightless bird needs ways of escaping or fighting predators. Otherwise, its species may be destroyed. Some flightless birds may have survived only because they lived in places without predators.

The big *Diatryma* had sharp talons, a powerful hooked beak, and a head the size of a horse's. Too big and heavy to fly, it stood over seven feet tall and hunted other animals for food. It lived 50 to 60 million years ago.

Zoobooks®

RATITE ACTIVITIES

by Carol Spirkoff Prime
Production with Linda Price

Ruffle some feathers with these ratite activities. Use what you have learned about ostriches and other ratites to complete the fun exercises on these four pages.

Picture This, Ratite

Get out your quill (er, uh, pencil) as you attempt this special picture crossword. Use the picture clues to fill in the words that go across or down. The five ratites from this book are all in this puzzle. Can you find and name them? (See page 4 for help.)

Across

1.

3.

7.

8.

10.

11.

12.

13.

Down

2.

6.

4.

9.

5.

11.

Parents, try these activities with your young children:

- Take your child on a treasure hunt to look for feathers that have fallen from birds in your community. Explain that the birds that have lost these feathers can fly, which is why they need stiff feathers. Compare these treasures with the picture of a soft ratite feather on page 5.

- Help your child create the body art ostrich in "Try Your Hand at This One." You could even create an ostrich on both of your child's arms. Then, review the information on pages 4 and 5 to give your child ideas about how an ostrich might move and act. Encourage your child to make his or her "ostrich" act like a real ostrich. If possible, take photographs of your child playing. Later, help your child write a story centered on the photos.

- Work with your child to count how many ratites appear on each two-page spread. If your child finds it easy to count up to 20, you might model how to count to fifty by counting all the ratites in this book. Repeat this several times, encouraging your child to join you.

Try Your Ha[nd] at This O[ne]

— yellow

— pink

— white with black

— black

Use finger paint, color[ed] zinc oxide, or makeup [to] turn your hand and arm[into] an ostrich. Paint the la[rge] areas of color first. Let [the] paint dry after each col[or.] Then paint details such [as] eyes, a beak, and nostri[ls.]

Frame That Ratite

Notice the pattern to the right made up of eggs and darts. The egg and dart design has been used for centuries to decorate buildings. You can use the egg and dart design to create a frame for your tempera painting of a ratite. Or, create your own egg pattern to design a frame.

Cut strips of cardboard to make your frame. Lay the strips around your painting. Cut them to fit the size of the artwork. Staple the corners together. Then, add your egg pattern.

Color the Ostrich

Egg Paint

Have you ever used an egg to paint a picture? For many centuries, this is just what many artists did. They called their egg paint *tempera.* You can make some of this egg paint yourself to create a painting of your favorite ratite. Follow these directions:

You will need: an egg yolk, water, vinegar, small bowls or jar lids, food coloring, soft paintbrushes, and paper or white cardboard.

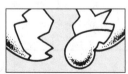

Break the egg into a bowl. Separate the yolk from the white. To the yolk, add a tablespoon of water and a drop of vinegar. Mix well.

Separate the egg mixture into small bowls or jar lids. Add several drops of food coloring to each bowl to make the colors you wish to use.

Paint a picture of your fa[vorite] ratite. Perhaps you might include several eggs in y[our] painting. (In paintings, eg[gs] are often included as a symbol of life.)

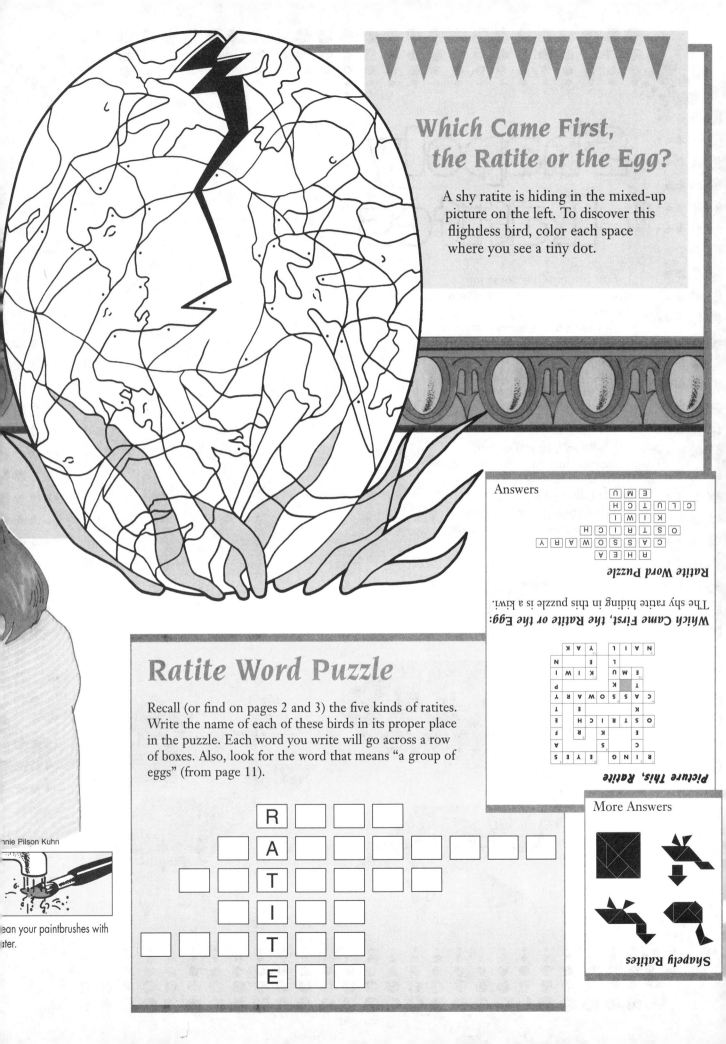

Which Came First, the Ratite or the Egg?

A shy ratite is hiding in the mixed-up picture on the left. To discover this flightless bird, color each space where you see a tiny dot.

Ratite Word Puzzle

Recall (or find on pages 2 and 3) the five kinds of ratites. Write the name of each of these birds in its proper place in the puzzle. Each word you write will go across a row of boxes. Also, look for the word that means "a group of eggs" (from page 11).

Annie Pilson Kuhn

Clean your paintbrushes with water.

Shapely Ratites

Can you turn this house into a ratite? In fact, can you turn it into 3 different ratites?

Cut apart the 7 shapes that make up the house. Then, put the shapes back together to make the 3 ratites shown below. Use all 7 shapes to make each picture. (You can make a photocopy of this page if you don't want to cut it up.)

Challenge: Can you use the 7 shapes to make a perfect square? Try to solve this ancient Chinese puzzle called a Tangram.

What other pictures can you create with your 7 Tangram shapes?

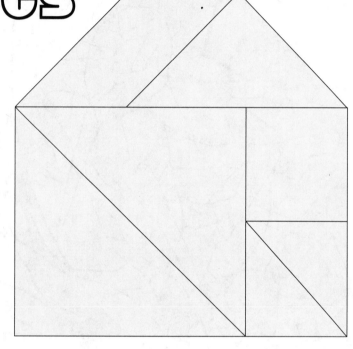

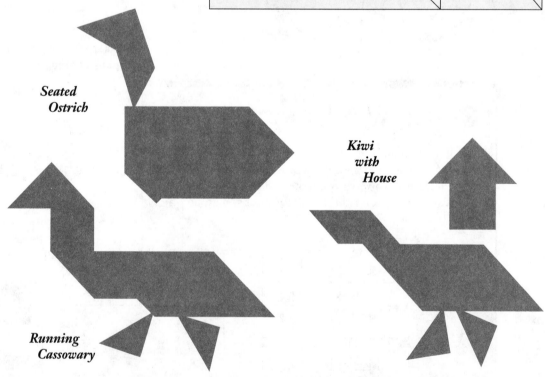

Seated Ostrich

Kiwi with House

Running Cassowary

The five flightless birds below once lived on the earth, but are now extinct. **1** The half-ton elephant bird *Aepyornis maximus* was the biggest bird that ever lived. It died out about 1,000 years ago. **2** *Diatryma steini*, a fierce bird not related to the ratites, lived until 45 million years ago. **3** The *Phororhacos* of South America died out some 10 million years ago. **4** The wingless moa of New Zealand became extinct less than 500 years ago. **5** *Emeus crassus*, a species of moa, died out in the last 1,000 years.

The moas of New Zealand were the largest birds of their time and had no wings at all. They started to die out centuries ago, but were finally killed off by humans. We know that humans ate them because scientists have found moa bones in human rubbish heaps.

Some flightless birds may have died out when they were hunted by meat-eating mammals. These mammals also may have eaten smaller animals that the big birds depended on for food.

For centuries, a flightless bird called the *dodo* lived on the island of Mauritius. After Europeans discovered the island in 1598, all the dodos were killed. The term "dumb as a dodo" came about because dodos were so easy to catch. But dodos were no dumber than any other bird. They just couldn't run fast enough to escape human predators.

Instead of flying away from their enemies, ratites run from them on powerful legs. Ostriches, rheas, and emus, which live in more open areas, protect themselves by staying close together in groups. There is safety in numbers.

9

Ratites are full of surprises. And they are record setters. Rheas and ostriches flock with grazing animals, eat watches and other shiny objects, and leave chick care to the males. The helmeted cassowary is an amazingly fierce fighter. Ratites are not only the biggest birds, but they also lay the biggest eggs of any bird. Their speed on foot is incredible. Some of these strange ways of behaving help ratites to survive. For instance, like other birds, ratites swallow stones and sand. These stay in a special neck organ called the gizzard. The stones and sand grind up the foods that birds eat to help them digest. So the shiny watch is just another gizzard stone to the rhea or ostrich.

Ostriches often travel with herds of oryxes, other antelopes, and zebras. The tall ostrich keeps an eye out for trouble, while the grazing animals stir up insects, small reptiles, and rodents—which the ostrich likes to eat.

Ostriches, rheas, and emus will eat almost anything shiny. Some have been known to eat watches, bottle caps, glass, locks, bicycle valves, and even alarm clocks. Some people think that these ratites can actually digest metal, but that's not true. The metal stays in their gizzards.

Cassowaries will attack men who hunt them, ripping their victims with their razor-sharp inner toenails. They can kill a man with a single blow. In spite of the danger, New Guinea natives hunt cassowaries for food and for their quills.

Like this cassowary, all male ratites sit on eggs laid by the females to keep them warm. (A group of bird eggs is called a *clutch*.) Sometimes the males even take care of the chicks when they hatch.

An ostrich on two legs can run faster than a horse on four legs, but it cannot run as far. After about half an hour, it slows down. Taking 15-foot strides, the ostrich runs about 30 miles an hour.

The kiwi lays the largest egg for its size of any bird. Sometimes a five-pound kiwi lays a one-pound egg. It isn't surprising that the kiwi usually lays only one egg per clutch.

Cassowaries are very good swimmers. They have been known to eat fish as well as fruit. Emus and rheas can swim, too.

11

Male and female cassowaries look alike, so it's hard to tell them apart. All cassowaries are shy, and usually prefer to be alone. But during the breeding season, they will spend time with a mate.

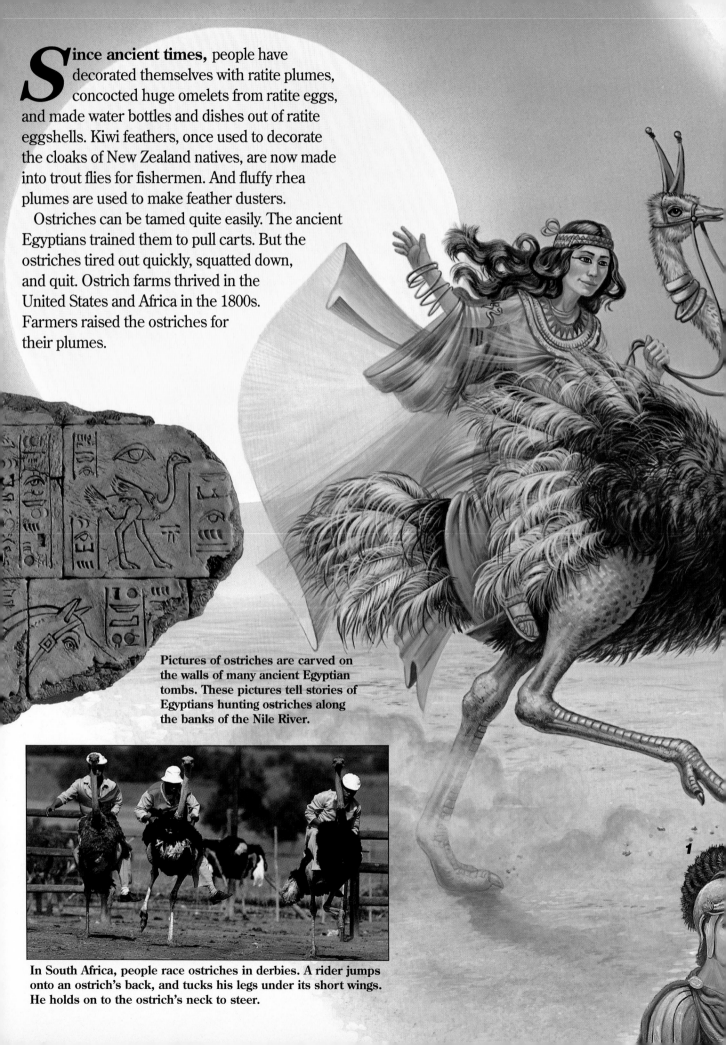

Since ancient times, people have decorated themselves with ratite plumes, concocted huge omelets from ratite eggs, and made water bottles and dishes out of ratite eggshells. Kiwi feathers, once used to decorate the cloaks of New Zealand natives, are now made into trout flies for fishermen. And fluffy rhea plumes are used to make feather dusters.

Ostriches can be tamed quite easily. The ancient Egyptians trained them to pull carts. But the ostriches tired out quickly, squatted down, and quit. Ostrich farms thrived in the United States and Africa in the 1800s. Farmers raised the ostriches for their plumes.

Pictures of ostriches are carved on the walls of many ancient Egyptian tombs. These pictures tell stories of Egyptians hunting ostriches along the banks of the Nile River.

In South Africa, people race ostriches in derbies. A rider jumps onto an ostrich's back, and tucks his legs under its short wings. He holds on to the ostrich's neck to steer.

1

Some South African ranchers have trained ostriches to act as shepherds for their flocks of sheep. Ostriches are not only fast runners, but they also tend to run around in circles. By running around the outside of the flock, they help to keep the sheep together.

The San people (sometimes called Bushmen) of the Kalahari Desert love to eat ostrich eggs. But they always leave at least one egg in a nest so that more ostriches will hatch.

Can you imagine how much fun it would be to ride a fast ostrich? More than 2,000 years ago, the Egyptian queen Arsinoe rode one with a saddle. We know this because an ancient bronze statue showed her riding on an ostrich's back.

The tribesmen of highland New Guinea like to decorate themselves with cassowary feathers. The dark, hair-like feathers almost look like fur. The tribesmen use the feathers to make headdresses for special occasions.

Ratite plumes have been popular with people for centuries. **1** Roman soldier, **2** English woman from the 1500s, **3** American woman from the 1890s, **4** Australian soldier, **5** African Masai warrior. All are wearing ostrich plumes, except the Australian, who has emu feathers in his hat.

2   3   4   5

Most ratites living today are not endangered, but their futures depend on us. They, like all things in nature, are affected by the pressures of civilization. They have been hunted for food, fun, and fashion. Their natural habitat suffers from pollution, deforestation, and the intrusion of domestic animals.

In the 19th and 20th centuries, three species of ratites became extinct. The Tasmanian emu was exterminated as a pest, the Kangaroo Island emu became extinct because of deforestation, and the Arabian ostrich was hunted to extinction for sport.

Although the Australian coat of arms pictures an emu as a symbol of the country, Australian farmers long tried to destroy these giant birds as pests. From the farmers' viewpoint, emus competed with livestock for food and water, trampled wheat fields, and foraged grain. The farmers fenced their property, but the emus jumped the fences. So, the farmers began to kill emus. Tens of thousands of emus were killed. Even the Royal Australian Artillery was brought in to win the Emu War. Surprisingly, the emu survives.

While still maintaining adequate numbers, the cassowary population shrinks as the rain forest is logged for timber and cleared to build roads in cassowary habitat. Feral pigs further destroy habitat, compete for food, and eat the eggs and young of cassowaries and other native wildlife.

If fashion weren't so fickle, the African ostrich probably wouldn't exist today. In the early 1900's, women all over the world adorned themselves with ostrich plumes. Hundreds of tons of ostrich feathers were sold annually. The species survived because ostrich farming became popular before the stately bird was hunted to extinction.

Today, most ratites survive because they reproduce faster than they are destroyed. It is important that this balance is maintained. When a species declines faster than it can replenish itself, extinction is on the way.

Extinction is a natural process that occurs over millions of years, with newly developing species replacing the old. When humans hasten extinction, it occurs over few years, and the ancient species are not replaced.

Legend says that ostriches bury their heads in the sand to hide. We bury our heads in the sand if we ignore the plants and animals that flourished before humans put them at risk. We, as part of nature, depend on these other forms of life. Without them we hasten our own extinction.

AN OSTRICH FAMILY